Cc

For Marlene & Bill —
Because good neighbors
are too rare a gift.

Warmly,
Wendy

Conspiracy Of Leaves

Wendy Babiak

Plain View Press
P.O. 42255
Austin, TX 78704

plainviewpress.net
sb@plainviewpress.net
512-441-2452

Copyright © 2010 Wendy Babiak. All rights reserved under International and Pan-American Copyright Conventions. No part of this book may be reproduced or distributed in any form or by any means, or stored in a data base or retrieval system, without written permission from the author. All rights, including electronic, are reserved by the author and her publisher.

ISBN: ISBN: 978-1-935514-47-3
Library of Congress Number: 2010920848

Cover art: "Mainvain" by Ester Fuldauer; www.esterfuldauer.com
Cover design by Susan Bright.

Acknowledgements

Thanks to the following publications for previously publishing the following poems: "Nonsense Poem #1" in the CD and print versions of *Between Quiet and Confrontation*, an anthology produced by the Shreveport Regional Arts Council, 2002; "Jerry Seinfeld's Favorite Poem" in *Barrelhouse*, #4, 2007; previous version of "Rondeau for my Wedding Night" online at *Numbat*, 2002; "Bitter in New Orleans" in *The Tampa Review* No. 37, 2009; "The Uninvited Guest" online at *Autumn Sky Poetry*, No. 2, 2006; "Sort(ing) of Sonnet" online at *Quarterly Journal of Ideology: A Critique of Conventional Wisdom*, Vol. 25, 2002; "Stanza of the Skeptic" online at the now-defunct *Butterfly: The Journal of Contemporary Buddhism*, 2001; "Couplets for D." online at the now-defunct *The Writer's Hood*, 2001; "Elegy" forthcoming online at *Big Bridge*; "Before Your Grandma's Funeral" in *Free Inquiry*, Volume 27, number 4 and "Conspiracy of Leaves" excerpted in *Poems Against War*, 2010.

Thanks to Pam Knight and Susan Bright for their efforts. Thank you to my husband for his patient patronage, and thanks in advance to my readers for your tolerance and open-mindedness. As Salmon Rushdie said, "Literature is the only place in society where, within the secrecy of our own heads, we can hear voices talking about everything in every possible way." These poems are not an attempt to hurt anyone's religious feelings, but only to explore the way forward for us as a single species in clear need of a new way of seeing our place on this planet.

For Brian, our children, and the world we hope to leave them.

Contents: Conspiracy Of Leaves

Telltale Signs

Eratos and the Motel Room	11
Apology To My Husband For Snapping Upon Being Made To Wait To Use the Shower & Get On With My Day	12
Nonsense Poem #1	13
Jerry Seinfeld's Favorite Poem	15
Rondeau For My Wedding Night	16
Bitter In New Orleans	17
Confessing Grief	18
The Uninvited Guest	19
The Garden This Morning	21

Plausible Deniability

Sonnet For the Angel Of New Orleans	25
Stanza Of the Skeptic	26
Good Lord!	27
Brother Judas	28
Before Your Grandma's Funeral	31

Inner Circles

Couplets For D.	35
Mother, Interrupted	36
Elegy	37
Birthday Poem For My Friend Whose Daughter Had Two Open-Heart Surgeries Before Her Own First Birthday	38
The Poet's Lament	40
Fall, Falling, Fallen	41
Associating With Azaleas	42

Whistle-Blowing

September Shipwreck	45
Sort(ing) Of Sonnet	46
On the Red River	47
Lessons From European History and TV Applied To Current Events While Washing the Dishes	48
Revelations	50
Wartime Generations	59

The Plot For Peace

After Weather	63
September In Sackets Harbor, Flags At Half-Mast	64
Cramped Quarters	65
Night Feeding	66
Conspiracy Of Leaves	67

Parting Shots

Time Contemplating Suicide	77
a posteriori	78
Permeability	84

About the Author	85

Telltale Signs

Eratos and the Motel Room

He coasts on cellophane wings as he parts the night air
and plants his barnacled feet on my balcony. Nearby
red neon announces VACANCY and bounces off
his black sunglasses and the sea-foam scales on his arms
held outstretched with a tangible confidence.
I open the window wide to fall against skin
cold as arctic nights. *You're late*, I accuse.
His voice rumbles into my ear, telling me
I should be happy he visits me at all, telling me
I should be happy he doesn't let my morning glories wither
or my ink pens run dry. He sings me a song of drought
to remind me of the wet season.

I trace the tattoo of a heart and dagger on his right shoulder
and draw a poem in hieroglyphics across his chest
leaving slivers of sea pearl beneath my fingernail
anticipating his departure. The ash from his cigarette
burns holes in my sheets. I sigh the decline of the West
but he just leaves me as he found me, empty
and overflowing with riddles, tapping
Morse-code prayers against the bedpost
rolling a salt-glazed scale
between my left thumb and forefinger.

Apology To My Husband For Snapping Upon Being Made To Wait To Use the Shower & Get On With My Day

I'm sorry: ever since that night you found me
in that no-breath, open-eyed state & brought me back
I've tried to see every day as lagniappe, an unexpected extra

but instead it's more like I'm living (forgive the cliché)
on borrowed time — all I can see is so much work
that needs doing, & any minute Chronos, that great creditor

will come along & hand me my bill. Then in the middle
of writing this apology, I saw, outside the window
just past that statue on the sill of Kwan Yin, whose hand

uplifted says "Be not afraid" of the medicine in the other
a little speckled butterfly alight, dark against the white stone
& I had to pause, and watch, as long as it warmed itself there.

Nonsense Poem #1

I've got a magic dragon I carry in my pocket.
I pull her out when I need some conversation.
She tells great jokes. She likes to make me laugh.
She tells me how she'd wear her hair, if she were human.
"I'd wait until it rained to wash it," she says. I tell her
how if I were a dragon, I would fly up to the balloons
to advise them, "Don't land there, not among the roses
or the blackberries, or the thistle with its purple tuft."

She laughs at me when I say I would eat bullets
and breathe fire. "They're awfully bitter," she says
"And you have such a sweet-tooth."

I tell her if I were a dragon I would dress in drag
like a reptilian James Dean and pretend the tail wasn't mine
when it sent cereal boxes crashing down in the aisles
of the grocery store, broken jars of spaghetti sauce
at my scaly feet. She says she'd like to see that.

She says if she were a mother she'd make her children
pick up all their toys. I say I'd like to see that, too.

If I were a dragon I'd catch shooting stars on my tongue
and kiss the ocean so I could hiss my husband's name in steam.

I'd slither my way into the chicken coop and con the hens
into telling me the truth about the egg, and who came first.

I'd grow as huge as a mountain and fly all the way
to the dark side of the moon
where I would scoop up the cold rocks
and carry them back in my beak and
drop them carefully on the world
as poems
in the rain.

continued…

And if someone who couldn't stand the chill
cast a spell to make me shrink to the size of a pebble
I'd wash my feet at the edge of a puddle
and put on my lipstick
in a convex mirror of dew.

Jerry Seinfeld's Favorite Poem

Jimmy Olson out-goofed Clark Kent hands down
ask any Tom, Dick or Sally at the newspaper.
Goofed-up, goofed-off, but at least his manners
seemed endless, yes ma'amming and no ma'amming Louis
holding doors while Clark stumbled into them.
And Lois with her sidelong glances at Superman
who never went unnoticed in his photogenic tights and cape
and that S that could have stood for *slick* or *soap*
every day saving *tout le monde* with *The Daily Planet*
serving to report it.
                    At night Jimmy dreamed
the clocks all stood still while Metropolis rocked
in waves of explosions and up in the fire-flashed sky
not a bird not a plane but Superman soared howling
with laughter, on his chest emblazoned his new letter: X.

Rondeau For My Wedding Night

Tonight I have no desire to sleep, though this day
has drained me: the family show-and-tell, the so-
whiteness of my dress begging for a wine-spill of Christ-blood
the pictures, the cake, the smiling 'til my mouth ached.

I should be empty of movement, after the gray
flagstones of the Sacred Heart's foundation swayed
beneath my satin-slippered feet. I should want sleep. No.
Tonight I have no desire

for anything but this, for you to place your hand this way
and unwrap me like a wedding present, open me
like a white silk envelope, for me to wrap you in the snow
of secrets and poems and thighs, for us to go
on never sleeping, for the time never to come when I say
Tonight I have no desire.

Bitter In New Orleans

It's happy hour down at St. Joe's Bar.
He's there with his boys drinking pitchers
of watered-down wine. Mary's at home

playing mah-jongg with the women
whining about housework and weeds
dollars and dime-store clerks

the jerks in line at Canal Villere.
Ever since Jesus took off nothing's been right.
The mosquitoes here bite harder than back home.

The antique shops offered a pittance
for His sandals, His old carpenter's tools.
What fools they were to leave, to heave

history in that sack and take off for some dream
of freedom and art. Joseph isn't even working
with wood anymore, and the cops here

are just as mean. But at sunset
church spires rise above the shops
on Magazine Street like hollyhocks

growing among herbs. Then nothing disturbs
the peace she feels walking at Audubon Park
watching the full moon flirt in the patches of sky

between the live oak's branches. But tonight
it dangles a mere crescent, spare blue light dusting
borders of solid shadows. She hurries home in fright.

Confessing Grief

Last night's rain remains in puddles
on the patio. On days like this I want
just to sit and watch my garden grow.

In the night the train's whistle calls to us
like a migrating bird. Through morning's mist
we track our dreams, searching for signs in the dirt.

The loose copper in our pockets rubs us
the wrong way. The early sunlight across
the waking sunflowers calls me to my senses.

Unbroken silence weighs like lead
in our disjointed hearts. I can't decide
if the time is right to tell you this:

> *Dad's been dead for nine years now. Still*
> *I search the trees for one lit up with grace.*

The Uninvited Guest

So Death comes to call; I offer him tea and
take his sickle and hide it in the closet. Its handle
feels rough on my palm. The foyer smell of cedar
chases away the moths from his empty sockets.
His robes flutter with butterfly wings.
He wears a necklace of hummingbird skulls.

In the kitchen the refrigerator's hum
drowns out his whispered words.
I pretend he isn't talking while
I sweeten the tea with lavender honey
but birdsong from outside
rolls in bitter on my tongue.

"In England, Shakespeare
had no trouble dying."
Death's voice rings out
razor sharp. I shiver
as my bare feet on the tile floor
catch February's chill.

Rummaging in the cupboards, I think
*Now that's just swell. Death comes to call
and I'm all out of cookies.*
That's what happens
when you forget to go shopping.
I make a note to write a poem later
on the back of a grocery list.

"God, that's just like an American."
Death's disgust at my lack of hospitality
rankles. The overfilled pitcher of nicety
grows too heavy for my weakened hands
and falls, crashing to bits on the floor.

continued…

Like my own Lilliputian minutemen
the shards scatter into a circle around him
barring the way against his heavy feet
while I, light with emptiness
levitate over the painted table.
Arms crossed, I address my guest:

"And now Mama-san will tell you
you presumptuous usurper
what's up: you will take your
rough-handled sickle, fluttering robe
and ominous whispering, and depart.
And you will stay long away."

Death hangs his bony head, smooth as an egg
(his has no cracks, as ours do, for through which
birth canal did it ever pass?), already missing
the taste of my tea. I tell him I must find out first
what can't be discovered. He laughs.
The birds outside sing *Hoc opus, hic labor est*.

The teacups dance to the sound of his leaving.
Pen in my left hand and rolling pin in my right
I hear his voice as he strides, resigned, away:
"Get to work, girl, and the next time I visit
you'll be glad for the rest." My refrigerator hums.
His parting words: "By the way, I prefer scones."

The Garden This Morning

Before the day's relentless scorching:

sunlight on sunflowers waving
wind through feathery yarrow
the glow of new roses opening
seed-heavy hollyhocks leaning

the red and green iridescent sheen
of the beetle scrambling
to escape the water falling
from my unkinked hose.

Plausible Deniability

Sonnet For the Angel Of New Orleans

We giggle like schoolgirls enjoying a private joke
as the local Shriners drive by in their little red cars.
Our old friend who saw spaceships and took you to bars
feared these beer-ballooned old men? Too much coke
too much smoke, too many psychedelic 'shrooms
not enough Fortran or time at turntables to keep his brain
nimble, too many borrowed conspiracy theories...his pain
refracted through the lenses of his too-groovy rooms.
His orange dreadlocks drew so many stares when they
tumbled down his back, you'd think he suffered leprosy.
But he loved being hated. He chose not to see
his limitless delusion. He cherished his path, his way
though it lost him everything, hanging with hookers and thugs
like a track star with a pulled hamstring falling for drugs.

Stanza Of the Skeptic

The adept-to-be practices watching his breath
with the fervor of a newborn sucking at her mother's breast
trying to drive a wedge between thinking and being
trying to unmask the iridescence of his very own buddha within
trying to peel off the common ignorance of humanity.
But what if this is just another spiritual pyramid scheme?
So many sitting in sessins like eager real-estate students, waiting
with minds on a good piece of nirvana (location, location, location)
the Master with his hand on the stopwatch, waiting to bang the gong.

Good Lord!

Christ's egregore is sore
from hanging on the cross so long.
He's happy about all those songs
but tired of the teams playing ball
and all the rest, bored to tears with fears
and holding hands in waiting rooms
and being called on for every stalled car
and hearing his name tossed about in bars
(and would really like to know
when his middle one became something
starting with H., or worse, F.).

Don't pray for me in Christ's name, please.
He's busy enough with wars
and football games in Texas.

He's mad as hell at Muhammad
who couldn't get his stories straight
and left the place littered with more nuts
than a whole grove of pecans drops
in a good year. And madder still
at the men who in his own name
drop bombs on the heads of babies.

Don't pray for me in Christ's name, please.
He's busy enough with wars
and football games in Texas.

He'd like to see us use our brooms
to sweep away more than dust.

Don't pray for me in Christ's name, please.
He's busy enough with wars
and football games in Texas.

Brother Judas

1.
The morning dawned still and hot, the sky over the field
painted like blood in water. The spare clouds hung
parallel to the horizon, bathed in an eerie light.
Watching the last star's glitter extinguished by the sun
he wondered, where would he find forgiveness?
The halter burned in his hand
as he made his way to the tree.
His hope deflated with every breath exhaled.

Across his path zigzagged the shadow of a falcon.
He would climb that tree to see farther, find an ass
pursue and tame it with the halter:
this is what he thought before he looked down
from the height of the branch. He couldn't wait
for some merciful wind to come sweep away
his regret and shame like fallen leaves
gone brittle in the sun.

One word kept sounding in his head:
terrible, terrible, terrible, terrible.
Was it fair that the Master had passed him
the wine-soaked bread? Whose vintage
made wine this bitter? His hand would never forget
the weight of those thirty silver coins.
His lips would never forgive that unhallowed kiss.
How long he had waited to feast at his Father's table
only to find there a cornucopia of pain.

He knew now he'd been born under the blackest star
marked from the beginning for this infamous end.
The green pines shouted their condemnation
each needle a tongue waving in blame.

2.
He'd hoped the messiah would lead in the old style
arms raised, calling Jehovah to rain terror
on their oppressors. With a word the man could make
a stormy sea serene. Why did he hang there so silent?
Now he was like a fire fully burned out
sand dumped on the coals, water stirred with the ashes
each and every ember cold. What does it mean
when a fair sky suddenly turns night dark?

We know we all wreak our hate on the world
but who will give free play to his love?
He wanted to get a message to the Master
but how does one post a letter to the sky?
How does the concept of *self* fence in the soul?
What border lies between breath and breeze?
How does the wind relate to the water?
How does the grass relate to the tree?
Never had the flight of sparrows
seemed such a miraculous taunt.

On what lofty height would he find truth perched?
And how could he fly there? What must be dismantled
to release this sorrowing heart?
Hoping for understanding here makes as much sense
as hoping to find an emerald in a pile of peas.

3.
He couldn't keep living crushed
under that mountain of doubt.
Grief frosted his every breath;
the tongue in his mouth told him: this is the taste
of death. Already his soul felt cold
as the granite of the tomb he'd be denied.

continued…

When did the noise in his head give way to this silence?
The wind in the languid grasses, the bleating of goats
from over that hill, myriad dragonflies —

all an eye-opening music. Around the tree
the grasses waved goodbye. It didn't matter that History
would paint his heart black as a moonless night.
He could feel his despair taking the long slide
into eternity. It didn't matter how long his body dangled
luxuriant in the sun. In his penultimate moment
he trembled like a clinging leaf, wanting
and not wanting the push of the wind, sorry
he hadn't borrowed a Roman sword to fall on

through constricted throat pushing out his last breath
in desperate prayer. How long will his betrayal
hang like a dark pendant in the minds of the faithful?
When they cut him down days later
his swollen belly burst open like a ripe melon
spilling his blackened guts on the ground.

Before Your Grandma's Funeral

What do you say to the nice old ladies
after your book-worming has taught you

the religion y'all once shared is just
a bunch of stories with suspect origins

like a poor man's quilt, pieced together
from the brightest and the darkest bits

of the generations who went before
also just guessing and imagining

while the earth shook and thunder clapped
and the stars whirled and flashed overhead?

Inner Circles

Couplets For D.

In the box printed with tulips languish unwritten notes to friends.
The telephone leaves no record except the bills that never end.

Soon it'll be time to turn another calendar page.
Next month we turn 34, you and I. Not a bad age.

This faceted glass holds water, not quite empty.
I wish I could bring it to you full when you're thirsty.

The pool-wet dress hung on the bicycle is now dry.
I remember washing your father's car under the Florida sky.

B. takes ours to the car wash where no one dumps suds or plays
    in the spray.
I sit in this wooden chair, wishing Charlottesville weren't so far away.

Licorice the fish lashes his furious red tail. I should clean.
I should wipe the dust from the cover of my mother's sewing machine.

I should sew a slipcover, bed-skirts, pillows, some other things.
I wish I could sew us a few pairs of wings.

Mother, Interrupted

Would that I knew how to clear this glass, which way and with what
>to wipe clean my vision so clouded with offered smoke and
>guttering wax.

Would that I knew how to relax the muscles so spastic with fear and
>passion I sleep like a crescent curled around a cantankerous
>black moon.

Would that I knew where it thinks it's going when my soul's elastic
>leash begins to expand in the vastness of space between our
>meandering stars.

They say each blade of grass
stands attended by an angel
whispering, "Grow! Grow!"

This I know:
My mother's birthstone is amethyst.
And: When I was a baby, we kissed.

Elegy

My father died at fifty-one.
Chasing skirts from north to south
his too-short life seemed lots of fun.

Handsome as Lucifer, bright as the sun
big words with ease spilled from his mouth.
My father died at fifty-one.

With accolades and honors they'd strewn
his path. Despite divorces and rumors (uncouth!)
his too-short life seemed lots of fun.

One night I found him sitting alone
in darkness, weeping. "They've found me out!"
My father died at fifty-one.

Two dames had thought they were his one
true love (there were more than two, in truth).
His too-short life seemed lots of fun.

Each woman delivered her ultimatum.
A few years later widowing the one made spouse
my father died at fifty-one.
His too-short life seemed lots of fun.

Birthday Poem For My Friend Whose Daughter Had Two Open-Heart Surgeries Before Her Own First Birthday

I wish I could write you a poem praising your beauty of spirit
that would fly to you like a bird from Heaven, or at least
        someplace near it
full of beatnik beatitudes, precious turns of phrase
images of green islands floating in cotton-candy clouds
girls with coral necklaces leading dolphins through the air
flocks of butterflies carrying postcards with news
of your salvation from the tedium of housework
and the salvation of all the world, young and old, paid and unpaid
a cessation of suffering across the board, no more illness and death
no more violence or famine, no more poverty of will, no more
        threat of soldier or police or lawyer
a buffet of bliss and forgiveness you could share with all your friends
who'd flock to you on a whirlwind of gratitude for a plate piled high
with satisfaction, and a slice of nirvana pie.

    Afterward you'd receive a Wish-Fulfilling Jewel to satisfy
        all your desires
be they for seven-layered strawberry cake or bamboo etageres
green beeswax candles or amethyst chandeliers
wineglasses etched with grapevines
(and cases of your favorite wines), patchouli bath salts
        dried from exotic seas
a collection of well-blended herbal teas
cedar shingles for your chicken coop
a copper pot to cook your favorite soup
long-handled dessert spoons in delicate silver
        baskets of flowers to deliver
antique boxes edged in scrollwork and sized
to hold the old photographs you've prized
or a garden full grown

islands of hollyhocks waving in the breeze bounded by
rosemary and sage, lavender and tiger lilies, sunflowers and roses
peonies, pansies, petunias, begonias, and a border
of the reddest salvia you'd ever have seen
like a thousand little flames
        around GiGi's upturned face
lighting the way for flocks of hummingbirds
that would dance to her laughter
like beneficent feathered faeries
on an overdue mission of grace. All this I wish
for you, my friend, but alas

there's only so much a poem can do. Next year, send a list.

The Poet's Lament

A canyon's silence I've never heard calls to me
like the distant laughter of children calling to a lonely child.

I am humbled by the presence of carpenter bees among the chives.
I wonder how to burn a candle at either end. The music of the muse

is muted by the total chaos of the playroom, blocks and balls
underfoot, the wild strawberry rambling through my herb garden

a sink full of dishes and a table cluttered with unfinished mending
dirty laundry on the floor and a mountain of clean clothes not folded

all calling for a different work. The wisdom of the ancients
calls down through the crowded corridors of time, barely a whisper

in the din of this century. I'd like to drop a quarter to call you.
We could chat about quatrains and sestets, watching the world spin

all the words we'd like to use when we feel free enough
but it costs more now, and you've got your own work to do.

Fall, Falling, Fallen

The leaves of the dogwoods now
almost match their berries, heavy
and red, swollen with rain.

Summer's green rage has cooled.
Spring's white petals seem an
almost mythical memory, made part

of the dirt the trees' roots explore.
Winter will come before we know it.
Before then the leaves will make

their own departure, to fall and rot.
In the coming months I'll be tickled by
your calloused hands and your mustache.

One day we too will become ground:
each rib, the ribbons of muscles
even these eyes and what goes on behind

all will return to become part again
of the seasons' dance. For now
we act as audience, tickled by each

change in the stage set
by the laughter of our children
by our own clumsy fumblings

in the dark, that all these years
have not made us expert in
each joining as glorious

and silly as the first.
However much water we drink
somehow we still thirst.

Associating With Azaleas

For Peter Meinke

I think of you, Peter, when azaleas bloom. I can't help myself.
At Sunday's brunch two pink ones, pale and translucent
sat poised in an old salt bottle above a ruffled carnation.

My children asked, "Are they real?" Him: with words.
Her: with fingertips gentle on the flowers themselves.
"Yes," I answered, not needing to touch them to know.

I saw the living architecture of their backlit petals
impossible for silk to mimic, and the perfection
of their glossy, graceful stamens, unattainable in plastic.

I thought of you then, and whether you'd been home
to witness the revelation of your yard this spring.
I think of you when I sit to be kissed by poetry

wondering what you've written today. I think of you
sometimes, at the end of yoga class, resting in Corpse Pose
knowing you'd be glad to hear I'm living life happily

balancing family and work, body and spirit, letting
my mind play in sunlight rather than entertaining the notion
of my head in the oven. I don't think of you

in the grocery store. I'm too busy chasing the children
and totaling my tab as I go. I don't think of you
while I sweep the kitchen, or fold the clothes, or scrub the toilets.

I don't think of you making love, or dinner, or washing dishes
except when azaleas light up my view through the window
above the sink. Every year I'll think of you, as long as they do.

Whistle-Blowing

September Shipwreck

1.
At the base of the cliff the gulls circle, screaming their hunger.
The white of feathers and the white of waves threaten dawn's light.

On this ship's deck cold as a monument's marble our exhausted feet
now trip to the sound of their calling. These herring they hunt

skip below the churning surface of the sea; with quick movements
they evade them like the safety of the port evades our captain

his eyes sewn shut with the sinew of rage. The rocky shore
calls him like a siren. The rope here in coils could make a net

or a noose. Our fingers have forgotten the art of knot-making.
The birds' noises sound to us now like children's mocking laughter.

2.
Your laughter breaks over me like the dawn
at the seashore, the light of the rising sun slipping
across the white breasts and wings of the gulls.
I am the herring they hunt, I am the cliff
where the water breaks again and again.
I am the deck, the bucket and the rope.
I am the boat, riding the waves of forgiveness.

3.
Where the waves recede
the periwinkles flap their

butterfly shells, digging in
letting the water deliver

the particulate manna
that sustains them.

4.
In the dark of the night yes we danced with our eyes on the stars
O! not knowing the music we danced to: just water cast against rocks.

Sort(ing) Of Sonnet

Falwell and his ilk: ugh! Now they blame
abortion and the gays for this horrendous attack.
Jeeze, don't it just make you wanna yack?
Some folks think instead it could well be
evangelistic invasion sponsored by corporate slavery.
Or bin Laden's ear in Satan's clutch.
No doubt we're better but by how much?
In lots of ways our culture's lame:
we want our bread buttered on both sides
want ten kinds of cake, want to drive
our SUVs to pristine valleys
to somehow sleep in starlight with no bugs.
(((((((YOU))))))) We send cyberhugs.
September ash tumbles like snowflakes in the breeze.

On the Red River

by an ancient swing bridge
going under we see black folk
fishing. Grandpa tells our children
"They're after catfish," though no one asked.
I try to not wince.

On the boat we're the only white family.
The Captain's white.
There's an Asian couple
and two black families, their children
mingling at the prow.

One of the moms stays under cover
as do I. We talk. She's from
Dallas. We laugh about in-laws
roll our eyes about husbands.

When it's safe for children to steer
the Captain gives our kids first dibs.
We take pictures. Later
after too much time for thought
he offers the others the same chance.

But when he takes us through the backwaters
and we're almost colliding with the canopy of branches
that could hide those snakes we saw before
swimming and sunning themselves in the trees

we're all together
scanning for the pattern
of snakeskin on bark.

Lessons From European History and TV Applied To Current Events While Washing the Dishes

My husband summed up a mutual ramble
while I did the dishes: "It comes down
somehow, to humans being the problem."

And it occurred to me that we
give little thought to what it means
not to live in a theocracy.

"Did you ever think about the Church"
he'd said, "making everyone read and write
poetry in a dead language?" You might

imagine my answer, that it was good
for Latin, but who knows what was perhaps
lost forever from other languages

and that it might have had something
to do with trying to preserve a
dying culture, or Empire

and don't forget, I'd reminded
that it used to be the social structure
was both political *and* ecclesiastic.

Putting away the dishes
I realized how nice it is
that how we worship and our freedom

have nothing, and everything
to do with each other and how
important it is that it remain so.

And how tiresome it must be
to live over there
and maybe shock and awe

could be doing them a great favor.
But I remembered an episode
of The Next Generation

when the big-eyed, big-breasted
counselor said softly
with just a tinge of irony

to a shattered panicked worshipper
who stood on the brink of
sacrificing someone else's life:

"That's the trouble with doing God's will.
How do you know what that is?"
And he put down the knife.

Revelations

Violence does not and cannot exist by itself;
it is invariably intertwined with "the lie."
                                    Alexander Solzhenitsyn

This has always been a man's world, and none of the reasons
hitherto brought forward in explanation of this fact has
seemed adequate.
                                    Simone de Beauvoir

1.
It's tough not to sound like a mystic when discussing the diaphanous
nature of matter. I mean, it feels solid enough — imagine hard iron
except it's not so solid, down past the molecular level. The paradox
of subatomic physics: that the sedate scientific method
could yield up such a wonder. Not only the light of the Sun
acts like both particle and wave, but everything: the petal of a rose
your cheek, the hard cruel curving beak of the red-tailed hawk
water, soil, stone: all somehow organized energy. Nothing's dead
at that level. Everything's in constant vibration. Part of the wind
moves through us. Breath is just the beginning. Part of you knows
this is the truth, though your brain rebels, shouts that this is bull.
You want reality to sit tidily contained in its perfect little box
but instead it runs amok like weeds in an unkempt flower bed.
When you agreed to be born, what did God offer as collateral?

2.
Used to be a war-plagued king would offer his son as collateral.
Daughters got worse, given in marriage, with dowries of diaphanous
fabrics, bags of gold, livestock, all to buy the king more power. To bed
her new lord would come, some man she didn't love, his will of iron
and if she dared refuse him, she just might find herself shut up in a box
prison cell or coffin. Thus the age of chivalry created a great paradox:
woman revered in story and song, but in fact no more than bull

or goat or piece of land: mere property. It's hard to believe this method
of degradation persists. In Pakistan Zahida Perveen's husband cut off
    her nose
her ears, gouged out her eyes, left her for dead, on a mere suspicion.
    The Sun
doesn't rise on a day a woman isn't murdered for honor. The wind
blowing around the earth carries a burden of sorrow. The rose
opening in my garden burns with the color of innocent blood. All
    these dead
cry out for justice; but the planet just seethes with god-mad men with
    girls to hawk.

3.
For amazement find a bird feather — it can be from a goshawk
or a hummingbird or a turkey, no matter, they're all on collateral
branches of the avian evolutionary path, their common ancestor long
    dead
but there in the fossil record — and note its structure, nearly
    diaphanous
made of interlocking barbs fine as hair, but harder. After the first
    bird rose
probably fleeing for its life, I wonder when they left their tree-beds
and began their migrations. Maybe an eon later. The course of
    evolution winds
around chance events and random mutations. It takes millennia to
    iron
out the wrinkles. To think all this started in chemical soup cooked by
    the Sun's
heat and stirred by mile-high tides...it makes me want to get up on a
    soap-box
and preach the wonders of science until everyone on the planet knows
this is the true miracle, nature with its immutable laws. The paradox
is that religion purports to be the truth, but it's just the age-old method
of control. It's not science, but what the imam and the preacher says,
    that's bull.

continued...

4.
Before, she loved that he was strong as a bull
that his gaze pierced like the golden eyes of a hawk
but cruelty has its method
and now the collateral
powers of jealousy and passion have forged this impossible paradox:
he'd rather see her dead
than see her even turn her nose
in anyone else's direction. Her diaphanous
veil couldn't conceal her fear as he took the knife from its box.
He watched as his hand rose
inexorable as the Sun
and watches her collapse, bleeding, on the bed
they shared, watches her grab for its post of iron.
Later, he'll remember the open window: her black hair blowing in the
    wind.

5.
Our Founding Fathers: Deists. They thought God built a clock to wind
and then abandon. Tell that to a Christian and he'll be mad as a
    bee-stung bull.
I don't mean the mystics. I mean the ones as dense as the iron
core of this planet of ours, you know, like those little-brained hawks
in the Capitol, who care so much about who takes whom to whose bed
but don't mind fighting a war using myriad un-American methods.
I wonder if they'd be so eager if each politician had to send his own
    son.
And I wonder why we are willing to offer up our ideals as collateral
in some misguided bid to secure a sense of safety. When smoke rose
from Manhattan, it marked our brightest and our darkest day:
    a paradox.
How are those dead heroes redeemed by these dead kids coming back
    in a box?
Rather than explore the healing found in forgiveness, we heap piles
    of the dead

on the dead. We think the solution shimmers before us like a mirage,
    diaphanous
in the heat of rage, receding at our approach, but the truth's right
    under our nose.

6.
Imagine what your dog knows with his nose.
On a September morning watch him sip the wind
while the light through the half-leaved tree branches and diaphanous
clouds shines on his wet, widening nostrils. He charges like a bull:
rabbit or squirrel? You can't know, your own smell-sense dead
by comparison: the price evolution exacts. We know the taste of iron—
blood in our mouths — its scent, barely. What we perceive creates the
    box
that confines our consciousness. In the eye of any hawk
works a second set of muscles ours lack. It seems a paradox
that our enormous brains could be so dull, but no. Thought's the deep
    bed
from which the towering and invasive flower of our species rose:
cooperation & community; speech & song; story & symbol. Then
    scientific method
gave rise to a new set of eyes. Some fear we've offered up our souls as
    collateral.
The same kind of folk refused to believe the Earth revolved 'round
    the Sun.

7.
What will we see in the light of tomorrow's Sun?
Of course nobody knows
the future, but I'd say we're headed for trouble. There must be some
    collateral
path we can choose, a different wind
we can fill our sails with. We need a better method
to measure progress, one that takes into account the diaphanous

continued…

gases from smokestack and exhaust pipe, that sees what rose
along with the GNP. How many bull markets are built on a bed
of somebody's suffering? We need to count all the dead
human and non-human, and acknowledge the paradox
of our technological wonderworld, before our ship finds itself in irons.
When we've cleaned out nature's storehouse we'll have nothing left to
    hawk.
Should we hand Creation, broken, back to God in a box?

8.
Alone, she slips back the rug, lifts the loose floorboard, extracts a box
which she opens as if it housed the remains of a saint. Her father's son
wouldn't have to hide a book. Asking her not to read: asking a hawk
not to fly. The dying flashlight's so dim she's got to stick her nose
almost to the page. It's a text of man's history, and she's up to the Iron
Age. While she absorbs the words her nimble brain spins a collateral
thread: the imam says she's worth half a boy, but can't explain the
    paradox
of her intelligence. Would Allah give a gift not meant to be used? The
    wind
covers the sounds of his steps. Too late she hears the door: she's dead.
She knew the price of disobedience. All that's left to decide is the
    method.
She passes the night, sleepless, serenaded by her mother's sobs,
    shivering in bed
until dawn creeps up the mountain, the colors dazzling through the
    diaphanous
curtain. Mingled with the morning's sound she hears the angry snort
    of a bull
and realizes, shocked, that she'd never before watched as the Sun rose.

9.
Consider the petals of the not-quite-aptly named Double Delight rose:
edges sun-tinged pink, and soft as the inside of a velvet-lined box
with a scent close to divine. A delight to eye and nose, that's no bull
but there's yet another way these petals can please (if you ask my son

way more important): dip one in egg white, then sugar. It'll dry to a
    diaphanous
crust, a heaven-nibble, perfect marriage of nectar and sap. His eyes
    roll back. Hawk-
like, his hand'll swoop and steal his sister's. He'd like nothing else to
    grow in the bed
the bush shares, not the eye-flaming Red Magnificence, doing nothing
    for the nose
nor anything else, just more of these same roses, but he knows that
    method —
monoculture — is no way to sustain life, unless you garden with a fist
    of iron.
Pesticides would render the petals inedible, and the soil dead.
Instead, we plant alyssum to attract hoverflies, offer butterfly weed
    like collateral
for the aphids, then watch monarchs and the flowers' seeds take to the
    wind.
That Nature, unknowing, knows what she's doing, is Earth's great
    paradox.

10.
In all its gore and glory, it seems the world presents us with a paradox.
Every part of the universe fulfilled its role in the play 'til the day man
    rose
to master nature, like Lucifer rising up against God. We'll wind
up in a hell, ours of our own making, unless we break out of this
    cramped box
our scriptures have confined us in. Before your birth God offered no
    collateral
because there is no God up there, though if you cling, bull-
headed, to the notion, no wonder you're in such a hurry to be dead.
Think of all that's beautiful, something as simple as the slanting sun-
light through the contaminated atmosphere, the river's banks
    red with iron
oxidized over eons, morning mist rising from city streets, diaphanous

continued…

between buildings scraping the sky, and wonder at the brain's method
for finding such phenomena so. With the soaring flight of a hawk
our spirit seems to hitch a ride: just a trick of the mind. Who knows
how long awe's been helping us survive; now we starve, rooted in a
      spent bed.

11.
There are days she can hardly get out of bed
oppressed by a blanket of sadness, trapped in the modern paradox
of the life of a Hindu widow. The stink of death fills her nose
as she waits to die by the Ganges, in Varanasi. This morning she rose
almost without moving, like a hawk
catching the wind
under its wide wings in their time-honored method
and took out the small box
that holds her remaining possessions: a diaphanous
scrap from her silk nuptial sari, embroidered with collateral
rows of jasmine flowers, a small iron
statue of a bull
(a gift from her husband), an unframed photo of her son
she never sees, back home, wishing she were already dead.

12.
How many millennia will men argue over what happens when you're
      dead?
Must we look in a moldy old book to know whom to take to bed?
The Bible's authors had no idea the Earth went around the Sun.
What do you expect to happen to a child's mind with this paradox
the clear contradiction between what they see and the load of bull
they're taught in Sunday school? Think about it: goodness knows
life is hard enough without forcing on them a mindset like an iron
cage. Let's hope this dark age is religion's death rattle, that like a rose
truth will soon bloom and broadcast its liberating perfume. The
      collateral
invested in the other world could be redeemed if we ceased to hawk
the Here and Now for hopes of Heaven. Every spring the diaphanous
green of new leaves, scent of living soil on a clean and gentle wind.

It's hope I seek to give you, wrapped up like a present in a pretty box.
But first we've got to drop the bullshit. To survive there is no other
> method.

13.
Waking with the cock's crowing every morning he wonders at the
> method
grief uses — the cold pillow, no smell of coffee — to remind him she's
> dead
like there's a danger he'll forget she's buried, rotting in that box.
For thirty-eight years they shared their dreams in this humble bed.
Ten thousand nights he was lulled by her breathing; now the wind
and the farmhouse's creaking make a nightly racket. Fifteen years ago
> their son
left for the city — a city job, a city wife — and now the boy's face
> rises diaphanous
in his disintegrating memory. Downstairs, fixing breakfast, the paradox
consumes him: for their mere presence at the table today he'd hawk
everything he owns, but when they did live here he let his work bull-
doze its way through their lives. He sacrificed happiness as collateral
for this future? So many missed chances for a quick kiss, a tweak of the
> boy's nose.
Even in old age her face had been soft, like the petals of a wilting rose.
Curse Time's backward alchemy: the gold of his past now just rusted
> iron.

14.
All matter began in the bellies of stars, but any element heavier than
> iron
like silver or copper or tin, required a cataclysm like a supernova. The
> method
used to make the stuff of the Universe: violence. Even the gentle
> petals of a rose
open on the end of a stem covered with thorns. Man carries violence
> like dead

continued…

weight, a vestigial habit evolution hasn't yet eliminated, though
      everyone knows
or should know, it causes more problems than it solves. From
      Pandora's box
it flew out with the rest of the world's curses. War, famine, disease: all
      collateral
developments. Busy making bombs, we're not baking bread; the
      vegetable bed
goes untended. It's woven like a thread through man's makeup. But
      look: a bull
will fight another bull for mating rights but would never gore a heifer.
      The wind
from the east broadcasts the stench of madness. Whether you see
      yourself as hawk
or dove you must know things had gone awry long before we invaded.
      A son
learns to be a man from his father. Cultures steeped in hate create a
      paradox
but nothing's insurmountable. Let's tend this hope, however flimsy,
      pale, diaphanous.

15.
And here, men with hearts hard as iron practice sanctimony, building
      a bed
no decent structure will stand on. We've boxed up our culture, one big
      paradox
and used every despicable method to export it, though it's not
      sustainable.
America wants to lead the world by its nose, wants to be at the center,
      like the Sun.
But since industry rose to power, the world has watched a foul wind
blow away the last remnants of liberty. Democracy's not yet dead,
      but they hawk
her crumbling estate. Diaphanous, Justice fades away, just
      forfeited collateral.

Wartime Generations

In its watery language the bay intimates
the coming nocturnal dismay. A child
watches her grandmother press fry bread
between weathered hands while her mother
watches the girl's fingers obsess with the frayed
hem of her dress.

All the mother wants is for her daughter
to discover and become her truest self.
She can't imagine the defeats she will suffer
the dead ends that will lure her, but houseflies
on the curtain remind her of the dark forces
that impel the rising tide.

She knows stones at the water's edge are slick
with a century's scum. Dead leaves cling
to the wet roof and walls, the garden fence
littering the landscape with this dismal confetti
leavings of the cloud's parade. *When did life
become a freak show in this*

circus of the absurd? She wonders what is necessary:
the crab, the water, the stones, the wind, the scum. All
these vagrants wandering makeshift realities, and poets
playing with histories, brandishing dangerous vagaries
juggling language like so many burning batons.
Yes, she sighs, *even those.*

The Plot For Peace

After Weather

The day we invaded Iraq, the rain fell hard here at home.

The sky was beyond clouded today
storming like my mind, dumping
enough rain to fill the streets
stop signs and traffic lights obscured
in the shimmer of water running down glass.

I'd like to curl up with the dogs
let their fur beneath my hands
take away the tension I've absorbed
from the world, but there's no time
now, dinner to get on the table

(kids to feed) a husband who needs
my attention not to waver while he paints
a picture of his day. My elastic soul
expands to embrace this, not stunted
by the lack of peace, not sickened

despite the sickness that pervades
this human experience like the rain
soaking into the soil: somewhere
out in my flooded yard I know await
the purple petals of a flawless violet

we'll find below tomorrow's sun.

September In Sackets Harbor, Flags At Half-Mast

By Black River Bay, walking the dogs:
Queen Anne's lace, purple asters, goldenrod
milkweed heavy with chrysalids and pods
dried brown thistle covered with down
in the fields, by the water, past the town;
metallic berries with a violet hue
the sky and bay two different blues
light and dark, kept apart by shards of land
thrown there once by God's right hand
when man ignored His last command
to turn their backs on the call to war
to live in love and fight no more.
The Thousand Islands: a lost paradise
winter will soon blanket with ice.

Cramped Quarters

The silence between moments stretches into eternity.
The eternity between silences stretches my nerves to the edge.

The ancient face of nothingness stares back across the divide.
The ancient face of my Self stares blankly at nothingness.

They said witches made candles from the fat of the faithful
so the faithful burned like candles any woman called a witch.

What would the spin doctors do with this latest turn of events?
What would real doctors do with no sick to pay the rent?

The heron on the log is sure of the presence of fish.
The fish aware of the heron survive under the log.

Our son is in love with the bare breast of Liberty
but USA's Liberty of 2001 keeps her breasts covered.

Our daughter's joy at jingling her bag of quarters breaks my heart.
Our daughter's presence makes me want to keep it beating.

I want to plant kisses like strawberries all over your face.
I want to plant kisses like strawberries all over your face.

We wonder what turtle laughter sounds like.
It's like the quiet of two children sleeping.

Night Feeding

Nursing hand-play in half-light, quiet
movement, open mother-palm explored

by tiny fingers, exquisite push and pull
thumb filling fist, slow, slow, and so slow

Time slows to a trickle like this tit-milk
when tongue tugs in semi-sleep

(between pulse-licks I count 7, 13, 9
though no number means *pull away*).

Future shudders up my spine. I know
I can't hide you from the tide of the world.

Exploring my mouth now, your just-kissed hand
grasps the hardness of teeth.

Conspiracy Of Leaves

He who knows only his own side of the case, knows little of that.
                                                                John Stuart Mill

1.
Butterflies drink deep nectar with tubular involuted
tongues. Not tongues, exactly, like what a lizard
licks with, or what you or I would use on a lollipop.
It's called a proboscis, and they unroll it while they teeter
on the edge of flower petals, then probe the part like a pillow
in the center, made up of tiny nectaries, a veritable estuary
of sugar-water, their straw-like tongues plunging, serpentine
in and in again, the outward pull impatient as an unpaid oracle
all the while balanced on six minute butterfly ankles
while what passes for a butterfly's brain juggles
the breeze and the shadows of birds, one enough to galvanize
miniature musculature into rapid flight. The fastest monorail
pales next to nature's engineering: a galaxy of atoms in one synapse.
They cling to leaf-bottom when rain comes down like strafe.

2.
After bombs fell down like hard rain on a village in a strafe
intended for our enemy, a man finds his wife's body involuted
in the rubble, around the axis of their dead daughter. His every
        synapse
screams impotent rage. Reason scuttles away like a lizard.
On the other side of the world, on a new-fangled Japanese monorail
station platform, a little girl holds her mother's hand, a red lollipop
clutched in the other, not knowing their neighbor's mind's galvanized
by hate. When the bomb blows up, the packed train will teeter
on the elevated track, then plummet, smashing traffic. Terror juggles
us all in its capable hands. Heads settle into grief like a pillow.
Dark men accused of no crime shuffle, chained wrists to ankles.
Terrorists breed like mosquitoes in this swamp of injustice, a fetid
        estuary.
Only bomb-makers and rebuilders profit. No oracle
need tell us the foundation of this conflict's green as serpentine.

                                                                continued...

3.
For protection from things that bite and sting a piece of serpentine
in your pocket's the trick. What talisman will keep away strafe
bullets pounding down like lead rain? In the desert the dark oracle
of sunset says it's coming, the buzz and hum of 'copters. Involuted
eddies of sand flow around the bodies felled, a temporary estuary
of blood. There's a human finger on the trigger. Which synapse
must fire to enable that contraction? I'd rather have both ankles
smashed than have a hand in such a massacre. The green lizard
slinks away, startled in my garden, more noble on its pillow
of leaves than one who'd kill children. Skyscraper and monorail
shopping mall and supermarket have us willing to juggle
right and wrong, keep our minds busy like a child with a lollipop
ignoring a splinter being pulled. We're too distracted to see we teeter
on the brink. Maybe it's time to find out what love can galvanize.

4.
Can love galvanize
words? Can some serpentine
meaning wind between them, push reason to teeter
and crash into compassion? Should a poem strafe
our collective conscience? Is a butterfly's beauty like a lollipop
to assuage it, or is my garden itself an oracle
prophesying peace? Here, nature juggles
the needs of aphid and ant, the involuted
leaf of the red canna, the green anole balanced there like a monorail
on its single track. Across town, at the estuary
marsh grasses act like a pillow
to cushion us from flood. How many synapses
have you devoted to noticing the grace scribed in a lizard's
slender ankle?

5.
Tie a silver bell on a red ribbon around her delicate ankle.
Let the tinkling of her movement from room to room galvanize
you into action. Seek her in the sleek curve of lizard
spine, the curl of cypress vine, each serpentine
tendril reaching for support a lesson. Let your synapses
branch and fire, connecting memory to desire 'til you teeter
on the edge of passion. Imagine her head on your pillow.
Don't let what they've told you intrude. Don't strafe
yourself with guilt. Let this be all: your blood an estuary
where love breeds its multitudes. Her name like a lollipop
rolled on your tongue. Is she a demon? No. Rail
against the lies you've been fed. Rail against the corrupt oracle
who first sold us that rotten apple. Human truth's involuted
around an axis of power. Just kiss her. Learn to juggle.

6.
Einstein felt sure God didn't gamble, but it's clear He does juggle.
He'll do it in a hurricane, in His bathrobe, standing on one ankle
while the clouds part and swirl and galaxies arc in involuted
spirals, and universes collide, gravity spilling in to galvanize
matter. Back up a couple millennia: go to a temple, find an oracle
to read the entrails of birds or the meandering track of a lizard.
You'll hear no talk of airplane, television or monorail
Jesus or Muhammad, but still, the clang of swords and the serpentine
tongues of senators'll echo the sound of home. Love's the lollipop
offered in exchange for the pain of existence. Our synapses
reach out in an orgy of connection, making sense of this estuary
of experience, breeding what? Thought? Our logic teeters
on the brink of no sense. The planet cries out for reason, but strafe
flies instead. Reason hides its embarrassed head under its pillow.

continued…

7.
A new widow nightly stains her pillow.
By day she learns to juggle
grief and the needs of children. Lovers' laughter strikes like strafe.
She remembers his lips on her ankle
while their daughter teeters
about the house in her heels. Alone, she holds the involuted
shell picked up on their honeymoon, down the coast from the estuary
where endangered brown pelicans mated. What can galvanize
a heart to heal? Is there a synapse
to connect *memory* with *absence*? The oracle
of pain makes its pronouncement. There is no lollipop
sweet enough to placate her need. Outside, the lizard
warms its blood in the sun while the serpentine
shadows creep closer. *He should never have taken that monorail.*

8.
At Disneyworld, riding from parking lot to park on the old monorail
see boxwoods propped and pruned: Sleeping Beauty on her pillow
Goofy, Donald, Mary Poppins with her umbrella, the serpentine
segments of the Loch Ness monster swimming through grass. Juggle
that image with this: in the shrinking unexplored rain forest a lizard
hunts, never having known the noise of man, not the staccato of strafe
nor the buzz of blades nor the whine of child for lollipop.
Both green beauty, but the first bears labor like a ball and chain at
      ankle.
The second requires only our absence. In the jungle there is no oracle
to counsel the species on the brink of extinction. When they teeter
no alarm sounds in the trees, though perhaps roots act like synapses
and the Earth knows. And perhaps her knowing can be involuted
fold in on itself, and if we see and love fiercely enough, we'll galvanize
her healing. Love the whole blessed planet; clean up your local estuary.

9.
Follow the scent of shallow water to find an estuary
where river-mouth meets sea and spreads wide, where no monorail
bisects the brackish horizon and sunlight and tides galvanize
the engine of life. Here, myriad species of fish spawn, tiny pillow
eggs settling between submerged stalks of grass. Wait, and involuted
clouds will bring rain. Trudge through muck. Watch for the serpentine
wriggle of water moccasin. Let it leave. Breathe. Let your synapses
light up like fireworks while the layers of your brain juggle
wonder and survival. Here, your sense of self can teeter
and collapse, and you become nothing more than your brother lizard
over there, eyeing you, sidelong. The litter at your feet's an oracle
and you don't like what it's got to say. Don't let it strafe
your sight; just pick it up. That heron's got fishing line around her
        ankle.
Everywhere, remnants of snack-cake, six-pack, cigarette, lollipop.

10.
Some days all she wants is to suck a lollipop
after riding past the estuary
to the lighthouse, to sit ankle-
deep in sand and roll it in her mouth, remembering riding the
        monorail
with him last summer. His kiss. The memories strafe
her, galvanize
her mind into a flurry of recrimination until the oracle
of hope soothes her, soft as a pillow.
She imagines tracing the tattoo of a lizard
with her fingertip, its tail involuted
around his shoulder. Hope teeters
knocked off balance by the serpentine
insinuation of newscast. *Insurgency.* How can she juggle
this need and that fear without blowing a synapse?

continued…

11.
In the structure of the clever poppy you will find not one synapse
yet it flashes ultraviolet light at butterflies like a bright lollipop
calling them from sky to do its bidding. Somehow it knows how to
      juggle
water needs of leaves and nectaries in meadows far from any estuary
with no guarantee of rain. In spring the thin stalks rise up, serpentine
like a cobra spreading its hood, lifting buds as thick as a baby's ankle
from which the wrinkled, paper-thin petals unfurl, to twitch and teeter
in the wind, sending light up like strobes. In Japan the monorail
moves so fast passengers miss such minutiae of beauty; the involuted
attention of the modern human denies the need. But perhaps strafe
would cease to fly if we felt the divine presence in poppy and cloud,
      lizard
and stone. Each other. Maybe we need to see with new eyes to
      galvanize
the change that must come. In night's quiet the head on my pillow
dreams of the world we would make with love as our oracle.

12.
In the near silence of early afternoon, listen to trees: wind's an oracle
urging stillness, insisting there must be some way to rewire synapses
to open them up to love. You sit upright on your silken pillow.
You turn your back on the distraction of housework, telephone,
      lollipop.
Distant dog bark, engine rumble, fan whir: you let them galvanize
your attention, bring it back to your breath. Your brain juggles
thoughts like a circus clown. You let it. You watch it like a lizard
watches ants parade. You realize your mind's as murky as an estuary
and as fertile. You wonder how you ever let thoughts of hate strafe
you, realize that grief and rage had wound themselves into a serpentine
monstrosity, strangling all sense. Each breath unwinds the involuted
selflessness you'd held in a tight ball. The pain in your ankle
calls you back, and you unfold yourself. You wonder if the monorail
will run on time tonight, bringing him home. Giddy with love, you
      teeter.

13.
Watch the spinning top teeter
as it slows, losing momentum like an oracle
as her brain clears out the potion that had held sway. A monorail
goes fast as it does 'cause a single track offers less friction. A synapse
firing takes chemical energy, to manage chaos or to move an ankle.
The less we think about it, the smoother it goes. Lay your head on a
    pillow.
Watch smoke rise in involuted
ripples. Savor each syllable like a lollipop.
Let the earth's serpentine
consciousness fill you, let it galvanize
your every cell. Imagine strafe
on the other side of the world blown aside in the wind. Juggle
clouds without looking. Let the drought-plagued river flood the
    estuary.
Love all your neighbors, down to the last lizard.

14.
In the pot of dirt planted with a mango pit see the skeleton of a lizard
the ants have laid bare, ribs as fine as hair. Its baby's skull could teeter
on the head of a pin. Did hunger kill it (my garden's no estuary)
or was it attacked by fierce fire ants that don't belong here? An oracle
might tell how it died, but most'd sooner trust an autopsy. We juggle
our need for truth and our desire to sing in an angelic choir. Monorail
medicine, Internet: gifts of technology science spawned, but so is strafe
and the planet's poisoning. Yet religion and its entrancement of our
    synapses
have fueled more than a few wars. The same need for the numinous
    galvanizes
art and culture. Once, on Andros, I nearly broke my ankle
staring up at the stars. We need to look where we're going. The
    serpentine
paths of science and spirit entwined would not make a bitter pill. O
the staff between, the straight path to love: medicine sweet as lollipops
for a world where pain and beauty must remain forever involuted.

continued...

15.
Look out! Like a lizard that green monster can steal every synapse
fast as a Japanese monorail. What do you envy? I've seen a lollipop
cause a kid's sanity to teeter, seen one lick be enough to galvanize
a little face to hate. Juggle these two possibilities: reclining, sated, on
        a pillow
a wealthy reader of bones. Or wading an estuary of sand stinging your
        ankles
with a burning question for the oracle. All you have of value is the
        serpentine
talisman. Under tent-flap, gold-glint. Involuted need transforms: knife
        strafe.

Parting Shots

Time Contemplating Suicide

No, I don't mean I've been spending time
imagining myself hanging from the rafters
or my blood seeping into bathwater like red paint

no, I mean, imagine Time as a woman
who's just had enough of our suffering
her watching the millennia trickle by

and us never getting any better at seeing
that she'll nearly stop for us to witness
the flutter of a hummingbird, the breeze

through an old rose's petals, or how cottonwood seeds
can float almost suspended midair in the stillness
of a summer afternoon, and instead just bitching

about how she flies when we're spending her
fruitlessly, and the way near the end of our lives
we realize how much of her we've wasted.

And so the august lady contemplates her end
imagines the apocalypse, when she'll fold
in on herself, bringing the alpha to the omega

letting the great snake finally swallow
his own tail. And what will we know?
Her secrets will die with her, her grave

lonelier than anything on or under earth
no one to sing dirges or send prayers skyward
no sky left, even, just ashes, everywhere

and no living flesh to wear them.

a posteriori

1.
just because
some old men

have always
loved palavering

inventing ridiculous
vocabularies

(way before Aristotle
long past Hegel)

we labor under millennia
of misunderstood metaphor

our reptilian
motor-brains

dictating
our relationship

with time
& each other

2.
in whale-fin
& bat-wing

hide bones for
five fingers

at some point
inconceivably

distant in the past
our shared ancestors

parted, some pressed
to return to the sea

some managing
to take to the air

& ours, remaining
in the dirt

to crawl like
bugs on a ball

curious: those minds
not confined to

forward & back
left & right

3.
just because
love feels

like a journey
doesn't mean

there's a destination
you never arrive

& if you want to avoid
unnecessary departures

remember
your partner's

continued…

personhood
that s/he

carries the same cross
(the human condition)

so follow somebody's
golden rule

4.
in the garden
columbine

rise from the soil
like little fists

ready to open
from whose palms

flowers will emerge
spurred stigmata

hiding nectar
deep enough

to draw the long-tongued
hummingbirds

almost as if
they were

designed
to do so

5.
like Kant
that old coot

(imagining metaphors
for space & time

had some reality
& could prove

the existence of god)
folks think because

the universe
follows rules

(laws that dictate
how matter behaves)

somebody
must've written them

6.
a lover's hands:
almost miraculous

dexterity, beyond
utility of tools

unbridled tenderness
open palms & fingertips

cupping ribcage
like a long-sought Grail

continued…

7.
it's not tough
to imagine

that matter
simply is

& always
has been

(forever entangled
with emptiness)

or that love carries
evolutionary advantages

it's just hard
to accept

8.
once whale-song
circled the globe

(their lyrics now
unbearably lonely)

& the language
of elephants, subsonic

carries for miles
their calls & responses

only our language
written as it is

travels through time
misconceptions

& imaginings
carved in stone

around our necks
dragging us down

9.
any idea regarding
ultimate reality

following from some
story or metaphor

(no matter how much
beauty or utility):

ipso facto
a *non sequitor*

10.
time to rise
from our knees

(bent too long
to the past)

& walk forward
to our future

hand in remarkable
human hand

Permeability

nature at bottom

re(lies)
_____

myth of division

               the knife twists
               ~~braided reality~~

(illusion of boundaries)

love carries away impurities
like water.

About the Author

A native of Florida and longtime resident of Louisiana, Wendy Babiak now lives with her family in upstate New York, where they've found refuge from the dominant culture of religious intolerance and small mindedness they encountered in Shreveport. Many of the poems in this volume are a response to that culture. She received her BA in Creative Writing from the Writing Workshop at Eckerd College in St. Petersburg, FL. She believes wholeheartedly in the power of language, second only to the power of love, though she recognizes that both can be misused; she does her best not to.